Enticing, Exotic L

Recipes

A Complete Cookbook of Excellent Emirati Dish Ideas!

BY: Allie Allen

COOK & ENJOY

Copyright Notes

This book is written as an informational tool. While the author has taken every precaution to ensure the accuracy of the information provided therein, the reader is warned that they assume all risk when following the content. The author will not be held responsible for any damages that may occur as a result of the readers' actions.

The author does not give permission to reproduce this book in any form, including but not limited to: print, social media posts, electronic copies or photocopies, unless permission is expressly given in writing.

Table of Contents

Introduction 6

United Arab Emirates Breakfast Recipes… 8

  1 – Local Chebabs Breakfast 9

  2 – Balaleet 12

  3 – Arabic Sausage, Eggs & Za'atar Toast 14

  4 – Breakfast Semolina 16

  5 – Shakshuka 19

Emirati Recipes for Lunch, Dinner, Side Dishes and Appetizers. 22

  6 – Ro-be-yan Nashif – Fried Shrimp with Spices 23

  7 – Assidat al-Boubar – Pumpkin Halvah 25

  8 – Batata Harra – Roasted Spicy Potatoes 28

  9 – Tabbouleh Salad 31

  10 – Chicken Makhtoum 34

  11 – Emirati Khameer Bread 36

  12 – Kabsa Rice 39

  13 – Emirati Beef Bowl 42

14 – Bulgur & Lentil Salad 44

15 – Emirati Biryani Dejaaj - Chicken Biryani 47

16 – Okra Fritters 51

17 – Middle Eastern Machboos 53

18 – Harira Soup 56

19 – Marak Samak - Fish Stew 59

20 – Middle Eastern Curry Rice 62

21 – Middle Eastern Cabbage Rolls 64

22 – Chicken Arseeyah 67

23 – Middle Eastern Lentil Soup 69

24 – Emirati Harees 71

25 – Chicken Kebobs – Shish Taouk 73

UAE Dessert Recipes 75

26 – Luqaimat – Sweet Dessert Balls 76

27 – Aish El Saraya – Bread Dessert 78

28 – Shaabiyat – Cream-Filled Pastries 81

29 – Umm Ali – Bread Pudding 84

30 – Batheeth 86

Conclusion.. 89

About the Author... 90

Author's Afterthoughts.. 92

Introduction

How can you create delicious Emirati dishes in your own kitchen?

Check out the recipes in this fabulous cookbook.

Can UAE cuisine's ingredients be sourced locally or substituted for?

Yes! Some of these recipes do include UAE ingredients, and where their substitutes are difficult to find, you can shop for them in world markets and online.

Many Emirati dishes are like soups and stews, and often, the whole meal is cooked in one pot. They utilize rice, which came to the region from Asia. Traditional dishes of the UAE include breakfast specialties like chebabs, and other interesting and tasty choices served with eggs, lamb sausage, cheese, or date syrup.

The mainstay of the Emirati diet is seafood, and it has been this way for hundreds of years. Muslims don't eat pork, so mutton, beef, and lamb are often served.

Upon arrival, guests are frequently offered Arabic coffee, known as Gahwah, and dates. At meal's end, red tea is often served, infused sometimes with mint.

Sweet dishes include deep-fried batter balls (luqaimat) and semolina with dates. Pistachio truffles are also a welcome treat for dessert, as is bread pudding, a wonderful dessert after a hot day outside. Turn the page, let's cook UAE recipes!

United Arab Emirates Breakfast Recipes...

1 – Local Chebabs Breakfast

Chebabs are a popular breakfast in homes and restaurants in the United Arab Emirates, especially in Dubai. It's a pancake meal of a sort, pairing well with eggs, date syrup, or cheese.

Makes 7 Servings

Cooking + Prep Time: 15 minutes

Ingredients:

- 2 & 1/4 lb. of flour, No. 1 (hard & soft wheat blend) – or wheat flour
- 1 lb. + 1 cup of flour, No.2 (wheat, bran blend) – or all-purpose flour
- 3/4 cup of sugar, palm (the same as granulated)
- A pinch of salt, kosher
- A pinch of cardamom
- A pinch of baking powder
- 2 eggs, large
- 1/2 tsp. of yeast, active
- 3 drops of food coloring, yellow
- 1/2 tsp. of vanilla extract, pure
- 3 heaped tsp. of milk, powdered
- 2 tbsp. of oil, olive
- 1 & 1/2 cup of water, filtered

Instructions:

Beat sugar with eggs, oil, powdered milk, vanilla extract, cardamom, yeast, kosher salt & food coloring.

Add 1/2 cup of filtered water gradually. Combine well for three to four minutes.

Add the No 1. flour. Fold with your hands. Add No. 2 flour. Beat by hand. Add 3/4 cup filtered water to mixture.

Cover dough. Allow to rise for an hour.

Pour the batter on pancake or chebab grill/machine. Cook till brownish-yellow.

Top with cream cheese, date syrup, etc. Add toppings like fruits, as desired. Serve.

2 – Balaleet

This is a savory but sweet dish, known as the most traditional of breakfasts in the UAE. You can enjoy it cold or hot.

Makes 4 Servings

Cooking + Prep Time: 25 minutes

Ingredients:

- 2 cups of wheat noodles (vermicelli)
- 8 tbsp. of butter, unsalted
- 3/4 cup of sugar, granulated
- 2 tbsp. of cardamom, ground
- 2 pinches of saffron – dilute in 2 tbsp. water
- 4 beaten eggs, large
- Oil, vegetable

Instructions:

In medium pan, heat 2 tbsp. oil. Add 1/2 of vermicelli. Fry vermicelli lightly for 4-6 minutes, till golden brown. Stir constantly so it doesn't burn.

Add sufficient filtered water to cover fried vermicelli and boil it. Once water has started boiling, add remainder of vermicelli. Cook for three minutes and drain in colander.

Add diluted saffron, sugar, cardamom and butter to pan. Heat and mix for 7-9 minutes, till sugar dissolves.

Add the vermicelli back into pan and mix. Cook and continue mixing for 2 minutes more.

Heat 3 tbsp. oil in separate pan. Add eggs. Tilt pan and spread eggs. When they have dried on top, then flip omelet over. Cook for 1 minute more.

Serve the vermicelli topped with the omelet.

3 – Arabic Sausage, Eggs & Za'atar Toast

This is the Dubai version of a popular Arabian and Middle Eastern dish. The eggs are served with sausage, a spicy lamb version if you can find it. The dish is finished off with za'atar toast.

Makes 2 Servings

Cooking + Prep Time: 1/2 hour

Ingredients:

- 4 eggs, large
- 4 sausages, Arabic if available
- 1-2 tbsp. of butter, unsalted
- Tomatoes, ripe, as desired
- 1 scoop za'atar seasoning blend
- Oil, olive
- Bread, rustic, to toast
- 2 tbsp. of yogurt, plain
- Salt, kosher, as desired
- Pepper, ground, as desired

Instructions:

Cook sausages in pan on med-high heat till browned.

Break eggs into separate pan. Add butter. Do not whisk.

Place pan on med-high and stir eggs. Remove from heat several times till eggs have come together.

Add yogurt to aid in stopping eggs' cooking. Season as desired.

Add oil to za'atar blend in bowl. Mix well. Spread over toast and serve.

4 – Breakfast Semolina

This is a complete breakfast that tastily offers sustenance for your day. It includes healthy fats and plant protein.

Makes 3 Servings

Cooking + Prep Time: 1/2 hour

Ingredients:

- 1 cup of semolina, med/fine – roast lightly in non-oiled pan on med. heat for 5-6 minutes
- 1 large, sliced onion, red
- 1 minced chili, green
- 1 curry leaf sprig
- 7-8 thinly sliced beans, French
- 2 tbsp. of chickpeas, split, husks removed
- 1 tbsp. of gram, black (like a mung bean), split, husks removed
- 1 tbsp. of ginger, grated
- 1/2 tbsp. of mustard seeds, black
- 1 tbsp. of chopped coriander leaves, fresh
- To cook: 2 tbsp. of oil, olive
- 1 tbsp. of butter, clarified
- 1 & 1/2 cups of water, hot
- 1 tbsp. of salt, kosher

Instructions:

Add oil to deep pan over med. heat. As it is heating up, add mustard seeds. As they begin splitting, add black gram, chickpeas and curry leaves. Sauté them.

As mixture turns golden, add ginger, chili and onions. Sprinkle 1/2 of kosher salt on mixture and continue to sauté. Add beans. Mix for several minutes until beans have cooked slightly and onions are soft.

Add semolina and remainder of kosher salt. Fry mixture over low heat for 3-4 minutes. Add hot water to cover semolina. Raise heat to medium and begin stirring. Semolina will absorb water and dry mixture up in 2-3 minutes.

Remove from heat. Add clarified butter and coriander. Serve.

5 – Shakshuka

Shakshuka is traditionally served at breakfast time in the Middle East. However, some people enjoy the dish a great deal and eat it at other times of the day, as well.

Makes 4 Servings

Cooking + Prep Time: 40 minutes

Ingredients:

- 2 tbsp. of oil, olive
- 1 cup of chopped onion, yellow
- 1 deseeded, diced bell pepper, red
- 1/4 tsp. of salt, sea + extra as desired
- Pepper, ground, as desired
- 3 minced cloves of garlic, medium
- 1/2 tsp. of paprika, smoked
- 1/2 tsp. of cumin, ground
- Optional: a pinch of pepper, cayenne
- 1 x 28-oz. can of tomatoes, crushed
- 2 tbsp. of harissa paste, prepared
- 1 cup of chopped spinach, fresh
- 3-5 eggs, large
- 1/3 cup of feta cheese crumbles
- 1/4 cup of parsley leaves, fresh
- 1 diced avocado
- Optional for garnishing: microgreens
- To serve: bread, toasted

Instructions:

Heat oil on med. heat in steel skillet. Add red peppers, onions, sea salt & ground pepper. Cook for 6-8 minutes, till onion is translucent and soft.

Lower heat to med-low. Add garlic, cumin, paprika and cayenne (if desired). Stir while cooking for 1/2 minute. Add harissa paste and tomatoes. Simmer till sauce thickens, 13-15 minutes.

Add spinach. Stir till it wilts. Make 3-5 indentations in sauce. Crack in eggs. Cover. Cook for 5-8 minutes, till eggs have set.

Season as desired. Sprinkle with avocado, parsley and feta crumbles. Add the microgreens, if desired. Serve with toast.

Emirati Recipes for Lunch, Dinner, Side Dishes and Appetizers...

6 – Ro-be-yan Nashif – Fried Shrimp with Spices

This dish is, as described, fried shrimp served in a wonderful spice paste. The family will smell the aroma of it cooking and be drawn to the kitchen.

Makes 4 Servings

Cooking + Prep Time: 35 minutes

Ingredients:

- 1 pound of cleaned shrimp, fresh
- 2 sliced onions, large
- 1/2 cup of oil, corn
- 1 tbsp. of bezar spice blend, prepared
- 1 tsp. of turmeric, ground
- A pinch of fennel seeds, ground
- 2 crushed cloves of garlic
- 1 tbsp. of lemon or lime, dried
- 1/2 tsp. of cumin, ground
- 6 leaves of curry or kaffir
- 1 & 1/2 tsp. of tomato paste, no salt added
- 1 tbsp. of ginger, grated
- Salt, sea, as desired

Instructions:

Heat the oil in pan. Add onions and fry till they brown.

Add remainder of ingredients except shrimp. Cook for 2 to 3 minutes on med-low.

Add a bit of water and the shrimp. Combine well. Reduce heat to low. Stir frequently while cooking for 12 to 15 minutes.

Serve promptly with veggies or rice.

7 – Assidat al-Boubar – Pumpkin Halvah

This pumpkin porridge is a much-loved side dish in the UAE. It's savory and sweet and usually served warm since it will thicken as it is cooling.

Makes 8-10 Servings

Cooking + Prep Time: 1 & 3/4 hours

Ingredients:

- 2 pounds of cubed acorn squash or peeled, seeded kabocha
- 3 & 1/2 cups of milk, whole
- 3/4 cup of sugar, granulated
- 1/2 cup of sugar, light brown, packed
- 1/2 cup of flour, almond
- 10 tbsp. of butter, unsalted
- 1 tsp. of water, rose
- 1/2 tsp. of cardamom, ground
- 1/2 tsp. of salt, kosher
- 2 cups of milk, powdered
- 1 cup of chopped almonds
- 1/2 cup of raisins, dark
- 1/2 cup of raisins, golden
- 2 tbsp. of butter, clarified

Instructions:

Add milk & squash in two batches to food processor, pureeing till smooth.

Transfer all of mixture to Dutch oven on med-high. Bring to boil. Stir often while cooking for 12-15 minutes.

Lower heat level to med. Stir often while cooking for an hour or so, till mixture has been reduced and has thickened to consistency like peanut butter, but looser.

Add almond butter, both types of sugar, rose water, unsalted butter, salt and cardamom. Stir often while cooking for five more minutes, till smooth.

Remove Dutch oven from the heat. Add powdered milk and stir. Use food processor to puree till there are no remaining lumps.

Add and stir 3/4 of almonds & all raisins. Transfer to serving bowl or platter. Sprinkle with remainder of almonds. Drizzle with clarified butter. Serve promptly.

8 – Batata Harra – Roasted Spicy Potatoes

This Middle Eastern dish really packs the heat. The harissa will spice up your roasted potatoes and make them an exotic and unique side dish.

Makes 6 Servings

Cooking + Prep Time: 55 minutes

Ingredients:

- 1 lb. of unpeeled potatoes
- 1 tbsp. of oil, olive
- 1 tbsp. of oil, sunflower
- 3 crushed, minced, peeled garlic cloves, large
- 1 tsp. of harissa spice blend
- 1/2 tsp. of chili flakes, red
- 1/4 tsp. of pepper, ground
- 1 seeded pepper, red – chop in 1/2" pieces
- 1/4 cup of cilantro, chopped
- 1 tbsp. of lemon juice, fresh
- Zest from 1 fresh lemon, grated

Instructions:

Heat the oven to 450F.

Wash potatoes and cut in 1" cubes. Add water and salt to large pot and add potatoes. Cook for 3-4 minutes. Use a colander to drain.

Return pot to stove on low heat. Put potatoes back in pot in 2 separate batches. Transfer them to large bowl.

Combine 2 oils, ground pepper and 1/2 tsp. harissa. Drizzle this mixture over potatoes, then gently stir, coating them.

Line rimmed cookie sheet with foil. Spread potatoes in one layer. Place pan in oven at 450F and roast for 10 minutes. Stop and stir in last 1/2 tsp. of the harissa, plus garlic, bell pepper, chili flakes and 1/2 of cilantro.

Return pan to oven for 20 more minutes, stirring at 10 minutes, till potatoes are browned nicely and tender. Remove pan from oven. Transfer potatoes to large-sized bowl. Add lemon juice and zest and stir.

Add cilantro just before you serve warm.

9 – Tabbouleh Salad

This side dish is a simple addition to a meal and easy to make. It's filled with the fresh taste of mint and parsley.

Makes 4 Servings

Cooking + Prep Time: 1/2 hour

Ingredients:

- 1/4 cup of uncooked quinoa
- 1 handful of fresh mint leaves
- 2 parsley bunches, fresh
- 1 diced small onion, red
- 1 diced tomato, large
- 1 diced cucumber, medium

For the dressing

- 2 tbsp. of oil, olive
- 1/4 cup of lemon juice, fresh-squeezed
- 1 tbsp. of honey, pure
- Sea salt & ground pepper, as desired

Optional additions

- 1/2 diced pepper, yellow
- 1/2 diced avocado, medium

Instructions:

Cook the quinoa using instructions on package.

Rinse the mint and parsley as needed. Chop finely in food processor or by hand.

Combine quinoa, mint, parsley and remaining fruits and vegetables in large bowl.

Whisk together dressing ingredients and season as desired.

Pour the dressing over quinoa salad. Combine well and serve.

10 – Chicken Makhtoum

I tried this recipe several months ago, and found it to be quite delicious. The chicken is accented so well by the vegetables and yogurt.

Makes 4 Servings

Cooking + Prep Time: 55 minutes

Ingredients:

- 2 chopped tomatoes, medium
- 1 tbsp. + 2 tbsp. of oil, corn
- 1/2 cup of diced onions, red or white
- 1 cup yogurt, plain
- 1 tsp. of salt, kosher
- 1 tbsp. of tomato paste, no salt added
- 1 tbsp. spice blend, Arabic
- 1 cup of peas, frozen
- 1 & 1/2 lb. of chicken meat, cut in four pieces

Instructions:

Sauté tomatoes in 1 tbsp. oil in frying pan till you have a mushy consistency.

To food processor, add sautéed tomatoes from step 1, along with yogurt, onions, Arabic spices, kosher salt & tomato paste. Blend till mixture is smooth.

In large-sized pot, add last 2 tbsp. oil. Once heated, add chicken pieces. Fry till they are golden brown.

Add yogurt mixture. Cook for 8-10 minutes over med. heat. Reduce heat level to low.

Add peas. Stir gently. Cover pot and allow mixture to cook for 18-20 minutes, till chicken has no pink remaining. Serve.

11 – Emirati Khameer Bread

Also known as Khameer Bread, this is a traditional type of bread in the UAE. It's a simple bread to make and is often served along with fresh cheeses.

Makes 4 pitas

Cooking + Prep Time: 30 minutes + 1 & 1/4 hours resting time

Ingredients:

- 2 cups of flour, bread
- 2 tbsp. of milk, dry
- 2 tbsp. of sugar, granulated
- 1/2 tbsp. of yeast, dry
- 1 tsp. of salt, kosher
- 1/2 tbsp. of baking powder
- 2 tbsp. of oil, olive
- 1/2 to 3/4 cup of water, warm

Optional, for topping:

- 1 egg, large
- 2 tbsp. sesame seeds or za'atar seasoning blend

Instructions:

Preheat oven to 450F.

In bowl of mixer, combine first six ingredients. Use a fork to combine well.

Add oil. Begin mixing while adding water gradually till you have a soft, consistent dough. Continue to knead for 10 minutes or more.

Oil bowl & dough lightly. Cover with cling wrap. Allow to rest for an hour, till its size doubles.

Cut dough in four equal parts and shape them into balls. Cover. Allow to rest for 15 minutes more.

Roll balls into circles 1/4" thick or less (pitas). Cover. Flip pitas on cooling rack.

Brush pitas with za'atar or sesame seeds on top.

Place rack and pita in 450F oven. Bake for two to three minutes, till top has browned a little and pita has puffed nicely. Remove from oven.

Repeat with remainder of pitas. Serve when cooled a bit.

12 – Kabsa Rice

This flavorful rice dish is easily prepared and easy to double. You can add a cup of green peas, if you like, to jazz the rice up a bit.

Makes Various # of Servings

Cooking + Prep Time: 50 minutes

Ingredients:

- 1 cup basmati rice, uncooked
- 1 tbsp. oil, corn
- 1 chopped onion, medium
- 2 minced garlic cloves
- 2 cinnamon bark pieces, small
- 4 cloves
- 1 tsp. of powdered pepper, black
- 1 tsp. of cumin, powdered
- 1 tsp. of cardamom, powdered
- 1 tsp. of cinnamon, powdered
- 1 tsp. of salt, kosher
- 1 tbsp. of tomato paste, no salt added
- 1 & 1/2 cups stock or water, filtered

Instructions:

In medium pot, heat oil. Add cloves, onions & cinnamon. Sauté till onions are golden.

Add garlic, tomato paste and spices. Combine well. Add stock or water. Allow to boil for 2-3 minutes.

Drain uncooked rice. Add to heated stock and stir gently. Allow rice to boil till almost no liquid remains.

Cover pot. Reduce heat to low. Cook for 12-15 minutes or so.

Remove lid. Allow steam to dissipate and place lid back on pot.

Turn rice pot over onto platter. Fluff it out and serve.

13 – Emirati Beef Bowl

This Middle Eastern ground beef bowl is an easy dinner that is quite tasty, as well. Traditional spices season the beef, and the dish is served over rice. It's rather like Kofta kebabs in bowls.

Makes 6 Servings

Cooking + Prep Time: 25 minutes

Ingredients:

- 2 lb. of beef, ground
- 1 diced large onion, yellow
- 4 minced garlic cloves
- 1 & 1/2 tsp. of salt, kosher
- 1/2 tsp. of pepper, ground, coarse
- 1/4 cup of water, filtered
- 2 tbsp. of coriander, ground
- 2 tsp. of cumin, ground
- 1 & 1/2 tsp. of cinnamon, ground
- 1 tsp. of allspice, ground
- 1/2 tsp. of pepper, cayenne
- Optional: 1/2 tsp. of mint leaves, dried
- 1/4 tsp. of ginger, ground

Instructions:

Add beef, onions, kosher salt & coarse pepper to large-sized skillet over med-high.

Cook beef, breaking it apart as it cooks, for 8 to 10 minutes, till browned.

To small-sized cup, add water, cumin, coriander, allspice, cinnamon, cayenne, ginger and mint leaves. Combine well.

Drain off excess fat from skillet. Add spices mixed with water.

Stir fully. Cook till water evaporates. Serve on rice, as desired.

14 – Bulgur & Lentil Salad

This is somewhat similar to Tabbouleh salads, except that it contains more herbs, more vegetables, and brown lentils. It's a favorite side dish in our home.

Makes 4-8 Servings

Cooking + Prep Time: 45 minutes

Ingredients:

- 1 cup of lentils, brown
- To cook lentils: 2 cups water, filtered
- 1 cup bulgur
- To soak bulgur: 2 cups water, boiling
- 1/4 cup of lemon juice, fresh
- 1/4 cup of oil, olive
- 2 minced garlic cloves
- 3 tbsp. chopped mint, fresh
- 3 tbsp. chopped dill, fresh
- 3 or 4 chopped onions, green
- 1 chopped small bell pepper, red
- 1 chopped small bell pepper, green
- 1 chopped celery stalk
- 1/4 cup of chopped walnuts, roasted
- 1/4 cup of olives, sliced, pimento or kalamata
- Salt, kosher & pepper, ground, as desired

To top salad:

- 1/4 cup light feta cheese crumbles
- 2 tomatoes, chopped

Instructions:

Wash lentils and rinse. Add along with 2 cups filtered water to pot. Cover partially. Cook for 18-20 minutes or so. Drain lentils. Place in large-sized bowl.

Soak bulgur wheat in bowl with 2 cups boiling, filtered water.

After lentils have cooked, drain water from bulgur. Add it to lentils.

Heat oil in small-sized frying pan and add garlic. Cook for 2-3 minutes. Add to bulgur and lentils.

Add remainder of ingredients, with the exception of cheese & tomatoes. Season as desired. Use feta cheese crumbles and tomatoes to top. Serve.

15 – Emirati Biryani Dejaaj - Chicken Biryani

The star of this recipe is bezar Middle Eastern spice mixture. It brings the taste of Dubai to a dish that is served elsewhere in the Arab world, as well.

Makes 4-6 Servings

Cooking + Prep Time: 1 hour & 20 minutes

Ingredients:

- 2 & 1/4 lb. of medium-sized chicken pieces
- 3 to 4 tbsp. of butter, clarified
- 1 thinly sliced onion, large
- 2 tbsp. of cashews
- 2 tbsp. of raisins, golden or dark
- Optional: 2 tbsp. of pine nuts
- 2 chopped tomatoes, medium
- Optional to serve: 4 large eggs, boiled

For the paste

- 1 onion, small
- 1" piece of ginger, fresh
- 6 garlic cloves
- 2 chilies, green
- 1/2 bunch of coriander leaves including stem
- 1 tbsp. of bezar spice blend
- 1/2 tsp. of powdered turmeric
- Salt, kosher, as desired
- 1/2 cup of plain yogurt, thick

For the rice

- 3 cups of rice, basmati
- 4 & 1/2 cups of water, filtered
- 1 tsp. of clarified butter
- 1 cinnamon stick
- 1 bay leaf, medium
- 10 peppercorns, black
- 3 cardamom pods
- 3 cloves
- 1 curry leaf sprig
- Salt, kosher, as desired

Instructions:

Start with the ingredients for the paste. Grind them till smooth and pour the paste into a medium bowl.

Wash chicken thoroughly. Drain well. Add to paste and rub paste into chicken. Let it marinate for 1/2 hour. During the same 1/2 hour, allow rice to soak.

Heat large pan and clarified butter. Fry onions until they brown. Drain onions and set them aside.

Fry the nuts and then raisins. Add to onions.

In same clarified butter, add chicken and marinade. Cook over low heat for 9-12 minutes. Add tomatoes. Cook for five minutes more.

In large pan, boil water with butter and spices for rice. Drain rice. Add to water.

Bring mixture to rolling boil. Reduce heat level. Cook till water is absorbed by rice.

Spread rice atop cooking chicken. Sprinkle top with dry fruits and fried onions.

Cover tightly. Cook on a high heat for 4-6 minutes. Reduce heat to low. Allow to set for 20-25 minutes. Then switch off heat. Serve while hot.

16 – Okra Fritters

If you have lots of okra in your garden or from a local farmer's market, this is a great way to use it. These fritters are a big hit, so they'll disappear quickly.

Makes Various # of Servings

Cooking + Prep Time: 25 minutes

Ingredients:

- 2 cups chopped okra, fresh
- 1/4 cup of chopped onion, red or yellow
- 1 tsp. of salt, kosher
- 1/4 tsp. of pepper, black
- 1/2 cup of water, filtered
- 1 egg, large
- 1/2 cup flour, all-purpose
- 1 tsp. baking powder, pure
- 1/2 cup corn meal
- To fry: oil, olive or vegetable

Instructions:

Mix all ingredients except okra in large-sized bowl. Add okra. Mix well.

Heat oil in medium wok. When oil has become hot, add batter in spoonfuls. Reduce heat to med. Cook fritters till golden brown in color. Remove them from the heat and allow them to drain on paper towel lined plate. Serve with dressing.

17 – Middle Eastern Machboos

This is a tasty, traditional meal with meat and spiced rice. It's filled with flavor and quite authentic to the area of the UAE.

Makes 1 Serving

Cooking + Prep Time: 1 hour & 20 minutes

Ingredients:

- 1 chicken leg, large
- 1/3 cup of rice, basmati
- 2 tsp. of oil, olive
- 1/4 onion, white or brown
- 1 minced clove of garlic
- 3/4 cup of stock, vegetable or chicken, low sodium
- 1 diced tomato, large
- 2 tbsp. of raisins, dark or golden
- 1 tsp. of lime juice, fresh
- 2 pods of cardamom – cut a small slit in each
- 1 cinnamon stick, small
- Turmeric & fennel seed spice mix, prepared

Instructions:

Pat chicken fully dry with kitchen towels. Use a bit of spice mixture and rub into chicken skin. Allow to set for 15 minutes or longer, as you prepare remainder of dish.

Rinse rice and soak it for 15 minutes.

Heat 1/2 oil in large skillet on med-high. Add chicken. Sear on each side till skin is light golden brown in color. It won't be fully cooked yet. Set chicken aside.

Add onions to skillet. Fry till softened, five to six minutes.

Add spice mixture, garlic, lime juice & cinnamon to onions. Cook for a minute more. Add and stir tomatoes, stock and the raisins.

Add chicken back into pan and season well. Reduce heat level to low. Then cover the pan and cook for 12-15 minutes till no pink remains in chicken.

Remove cinnamon stick. Discard. Remove chicken. Set it aside.

Stir rice into pan mixture. Raise heat to med-low. Leave uncovered and simmer for 10-12 minutes, till most water is evaporated. Reduce heat level to low. Cover pan. Cook for 15 minutes more.

As rice cooks, heat remaining oil in separate pan on med-high. Add chicken when it has heated. Cook, turning regularly, till chicken is a darker brown in color and charred a little. You want a crispy skin.

Add rice to plate. Add chicken over rice. Use mint or parsley to garnish if you like. Serve.

18 – Harira Soup

The base of this soup originated in Morocco. It has spread throughout the Middle East, including the UAE. It's especially tasty and a comfort food during cold weather.

Makes 4 Servings

Cooking + Prep Time: 2 hours & 45 minutes

Ingredients:

- 1 lb. of lamb, cubed or ground – you can use beef if you prefer
- 1 tsp. of turmeric, ground
- 1/2 tsp. of pepper, black
- 1/2 tsp. of ginger, ground
- 1 tsp. of cinnamon, ground
- 2 stock cubes
- 1 pinch pepper, cayenne
- 3 tbsp. oil, cooking
- 1 chopped onion, large
- 2 chopped tomatoes, medium
- 1/2 cup of chopped cilantro, fresh
- 8 cups water, filtered
- 3/4 cup of lentils, brown – you could also use split green peas or mung beans
- 1 x 15-ounce can of drained garbanzo beans
- 1 cup of noodles, vermicelli
- 1 fresh lemon, juice only
- Optional: 2 beaten eggs, large

Instructions:

In large pot, heat oil. Sauté lamb till browned nicely. Add onions. Sauté till they are transparent and soft. Add tomatoes, lentils, stock cubes and spices. Combine well.

Add water to pot. Bring to boil. Simmer till lamb becomes tender, two hours or so.

Add vermicelli and garbanzo beans. Bring to boil. Simmer for 1/2 hour.

Stir in eggs and lemon juice. Cook for 1-2 minutes. Serve hot.

19 – Marak Samak - Fish Stew

This tasty stew is made slightly differently, depending on the country in the Middle East where it is being made. It is sometimes served like curry and sometimes more like a stew.

Makes 4 Servings

Cooking + Prep Time: 1 & 1/2 hour + 20 minutes marinating time

Ingredients:

- 2 & 1/4 lb. of white fish – slice in 3" slices

For marinade

- 3 minced garlic cloves
- 1 tbsp. of spice blend, Arabian
- 1" cube grated ginger, fresh
- 1 tsp. of salt, sea
- 1 fresh lemon, juice only

For stew

- 2 tbsp. of oil, corn
- 1 cup of finely chopped onions, white or yellow
- 2 minced garlic cloves
- 1 tsp. of grated ginger, fresh
- 1 skinned, seeded, chopped tomato, large
- 1-2 chilies, green
- 1 tsp. spice mix, Arabian
- 2 stock cubes
- 1 tsp. of powdered turmeric
- 1 tsp. of powdered cumin
- 1 tsp. of powdered cinnamon
- 2" cube of tamarind seeds, dried – soak it in heated water
- 2 tbsp. of tomato paste, no salt added
- 6 cups of water, filtered

- 2 black lemons, dried
- 1/2 cup of chopped cilantro, fresh
- To fry: 1/4 cup oil, corn

Instructions:

Mix ingredients for marinade together. Rub thoroughly into fish. Set fish aside for 20 minutes. Place tamarind seeds to soak.

Heat oil in wok. Add marinated pieces of fish. Fry lightly till golden brown in color. It will finish cooking later. Drain fish on paper towel-lined plate.

Use your hands to separate tamarind seeds while soaking. Drain them into separate bowl. Save their soaking water and discard the seeds.

In med. pot, heat 2 tbsp. oil. Add onions. Sauté till translucent and soft.

Add green chili, tomatoes, ginger and garlic. Stir till tomatoes are soft.

Add spice blend, stock cubes, cumin, turmeric, dried lemons & cinnamon.

Add water, tomato paste and juice from tamarind seeds. Stir well. Bring to boil and simmer for 20-25 minutes.

Add cilantro and fried chunks of fish. Cover pot. Simmer for 10 minutes more. Serve.

20 – Middle Eastern Curry Rice

This recipe is easy to make and yields lovely, sautéed vegetables with curry-flavored rice. There aren't many ingredients, and everyone loves the combination of flavors.

Makes 4 Servings

Cooking + Prep Time: 35 minutes

Ingredients:

- 1 cup of rice, long grain
- 16 oz. of broth, vegetable, low sodium
- 1 bell pepper, green
- 1/2 cup of diced onion, white
- 1/2 tsp. of salt, kosher
- 1/4 tsp. of pepper, black
- 1/2 cup of peas, frozen or fresh
- 1 tsp. of curry powder
- For serving: 2 cut green onions, fresh

Instructions:

Cook the rice using package directions, in broth.

Sauté chopped onions and bell pepper in large skillet in 1 tbsp. water for 10-15 minutes, till onion has turned transparent.

Stir in curry powder, kosher salt & black pepper. Stir while simmering on low heat for 4-6 minutes.

Add cooked rice & peas to skillet. Heat fully through.

Transfer curry rice to plates. Sprinkle with chopped green onions and serve.

21 – Middle Eastern Cabbage Rolls

This dish is a wonderful choice for your weekly repertoire. The cabbage leaves are filled with lentils and brown rice, and served with tahini, pine nuts, lemon, and mint.

Makes 4 Servings

Cooking + Prep Time: 1 hour & 25 minutes

Ingredients:

- 16 cabbage leaves, large – trim the stems
- 1 tbsp. of oil, rapeseed
- 2 finely chopped onions, large
- 1 & 1/2 oz. of pine nuts
- 5 & 1/3 oz. of basmati rice, brown
- 1 tbsp. of coriander, ground
- 1 tbsp. of cumin, ground
- 1 & 1/2 tsp. of cinnamon, ground
- 1 & 1/2 tbsp. of bouillon powder, vegetable
- 1 x 14-oz. can of drained lentils, green
- 1 zested, juiced lemon, fresh
- 4 tbsp. of mint, chopped
- 2 tbsp. of tahini
- 1 grated clove of garlic

For salad

- 6 sliced tomatoes, ripe
- 1/4 slice cucumber, medium
- 12 pitted, sliced olives, kalamata
- 1 tbsp. of mint, chopped

Instructions:

Bring large pot of filtered water to boil. Add cabbage leaves. Weigh them down in water with a heavy spoon or ladle. Boil leaves for four minutes. Drain well and reserve the water.

Heat oil in non-stick frying pan. Reserve 2 tbsp. onions. Fry remainder till barely golden, 8-10 minutes. Stir in pine nuts. Cook till they begin to show color. Add rice and spices.

Add 2 cups of reserved cabbage water. Stir in bouillon powder and cover. Cook till liquid has been absorbed and rice is nearly tender, about 15 minutes. Stir in lentils, mint and lemon zest.

Heat oven to 350F.

Add spoon full of rice onto middle of cabbage leaf. Roll leaf up. Place in shallow baking dish. Repeat this step with remainder of leaves and rice. Cover baking dish. Bake in 350F oven for 1/2 hour till rice becomes fully tender.

Combine 3 tbsp. water with garlic, lemon juice and tahini. Mix reserved onions with salad ingredients. Serve cabbage rolls with salad.

22 – Chicken Arseeyah

This is a hearty yet simple chicken and rice dish. It's often considered to be one of the greatest comfort foods in the UAE, even for children who don't enjoy some of their spicier dishes.

Makes Various # of Servings

Cooking + Prep Time: 1 hour & 25 minutes

Ingredients:

- 2 cups of rice, short grain
- 2 & 1/4 lb. chicken breast
- 8 cups water, filtered
- 1 lg. piece cinnamon bark
- 1 tsp. of cardamom, ground
- 2 tsp. of salt, kosher
- 1/4 tsp. of powdered pepper, black
- Melted butter, clarified

Instructions:

In medium pot, add water, cinnamon bark and chicken. Boil chicken for an hour, till it falls off its bones. Skim scum from top of pot. Strain chicken. Reserve broth.

Cool and debone chicken. Finely chop in pieces.

In larger pot, add strained broth, chicken pieces, rice, kosher salt, pepper powder & cardamom powder and stir.

Cover pot and bring to boil. Simmer over low heat for 1/2 hour. Stir every 10 minutes.

Turn heat off. Remove pot lid and allow steam to escape. Season as desired.

In mixer on High setting, mix chicken and rice mixture till they meld into one another. Serve hot.

23 – Middle Eastern Lentil Soup

This lentil soup recipe is a high protein dish that's sure to please. The meatless meal or side dish is a favorite, especially on gloomy or cold days.

Makes 6 Servings

Cooking + Prep Time: 55 minutes

Ingredients:

- 1 tbsp. of oil, vegetable
- 1 chopped onion, medium
- 2 finely chopped garlic cloves
- 1 & 1/2 cups lentils, yellow or red
- 8 cups stock, vegetable or chicken
- 1 tsp. of turmeric, ground
- 1 & 1/2 tsp. of cumin, ground
- A handful chopped parsley, flat-leaf
- 1/2 fresh lemon, juice only

Instructions:

Heat vegetable oil in medium pan. Fry onions gently for five minutes.

Add garlic, cumin and turmeric. Continue to cook for several more minutes.

Stir in lentils and add stock. Cook while stirring occasionally for 35-40 minutes. Make sure lentils don't stick to the pan.

Stir in the lemon juice. Add parsley. Cook for a couple more minutes. Serve with crusty bread, if you like.

24 – Emirati Harees

"Harees" is the local UAE term for wheatberries. This dish is a thick type of porridge that comes together easily, with a few ingredients but lots of flavor.

Makes 4 Servings

Cooking + Prep Time: 1 & 1/2 hour

Ingredients:

- 2 lb. of meat – chicken & lamb work well
- 3 cups oatmeal, plain
- 1 chopped onion, small
- 1 cinnamon stick, small
- 6 cups water, filtered
- 1 tbsp. salt, kosher
- 1/4 tsp. pepper, black
- 1/2 tsp. powdered cinnamon
- 1/4 – 1/2 cup unsalted butter, melted

Instructions:

Add water to large-sized pot. Add meat, cinnamon and onions. Bring mixture to boil. Cook till quite tender.

Remove the meat and debone, if you used a bone-in meat. Place meat minus bones in food processor. Blitz for several seconds till shredded well.

Drain meat stock into large-sized pot. Add shredded meat, along with oats, cinnamon, salt & ground pepper. Use a whisk to stir.

Bring to boil, checking every 5-10 minutes. Stir while checking. Add additional water as needed. Cook for 40-45 minutes. Add butter. Stir, then serve.

25 – Chicken Kebobs – Shish Taouk

This Emirati recipe shows the way to prepare the spicy marinade and cook the chicken used in the kebobs. You can use your favorite veggies to add to the skewers, if you like.

Makes 6-8 Servings

Cooking + Prep Time: 30 minutes + 2-8 hours marinating time

Ingredients:

- 2 pounds of chicken breast, de-boned, cubed
- 3 tbsp. of lemon juice, fresh
- 1 tbsp. of oil, olive
- 2 finely chopped garlic cloves
- 1/4 tsp. of cumin, ground
- 1/2 tsp. of pepper, black
- 1/8 tsp. of cayenne, ground

Instructions:

Combine all the ingredients in medium-sized bowl.

Cover the bowl and set in refrigerator. Marinate for 2 hours or overnight.

Place 5+/- pieces of chicken on each skewer.

Grill on med. till done, about 15 minutes. Turn skewers as you cook. There should be no pink remaining.

Serve with a salad or rice and bread, if you like.

UAE Dessert Recipes...

26 – Luqaimat – Sweet Dessert Balls

These sweet balls are eaten by hand, and there is usually finger-licking accompanying them being devoured. The recipe is quick but they disappear even quicker.

Makes 5 Servings

Cooking + Prep Time: 50 minutes

Ingredients:

- 1 cup of flour, all-purpose
- 3 tbsp. of powdered milk
- A pinch kosher salt
- A pinch sugar, granulated
- 1/4 tbsp. of yeast
- 1/2 cup of water, filtered
- 1/2 quart of oil, sunflower or canola

For sugary syrup

- 2 cups of sugar, granulated
- 1 & 1/2 cups of water, filtered
- 1 tsp. of lemon juice, fresh

Instructions:

Add lime juice and sugar to water in a medium pan. Boil for a few minutes, till they form syrup. Allow to cool.

Combine milk powder, flour, sugar, salt & yeast to create the dough. Add water as you mix and knead fully. Allow to rest for 12-15 minutes so it can rise.

Cut dough in roughly 1 tbsp. size balls. Deep fry in oil till they are golden brown, then remove them and let them cool down a little.

Add fried, golden pieces to syrup. Serve.

27 – Aish El Saraya – Bread Dessert

This dessert will win over even those family members who aren't wild about sweets. It's a soft, creamy pudding filled with dried fruits.

Makes 5-6 Servings

Cooking + Prep Time: 45 minutes + 5-8 hours refrigeration time

Ingredients:

For the syrup:

- 1 cup of water, filtered
- 1 tbsp. of rose water, if available
- 1 tbsp. water, orange blossom, if available
- 1 tbsp. of lemon juice, fresh
- 1 cup of sugar, palm or granulated

For the custard

- 2 & 1/8 cup milk, 2%
- 14 ounces of sweetened milk, condensed
- 1 & 1/4 cup of whipping cream, heavy
- 1 to 2 tsp. of rose water, if available
- 1 to 2 tsp. of water, orange blossom, if available
- 5 tbsp. of flour, corn
- 30 small "biscuits" of twice cooked, toasted bread, called rusks
- For garnishing: chopped pistachios

Instructions:

Place rusks in square baking dish.

To prepare syrup, mix water, lemon juice and sugar in pan. Heat on med. Once sugar melts, add orange blossom water and rose water, if available. Remove pan from heat. Let it cool a bit.

Pour syrup over rusk in baking dish. Allow syrup to soak in. Line a second layer of the rusks. Add syrup atop that layer. Allow syrup to soak in nicely.

To prepare custard, mix 1/2 of milk with flour. Combine well.

Combine corn flour, condensed milk, cream and remainder of milk together in heavy pan on med. heat. Stir till it becomes thick and smooth. Once it has thickened, add orange blossom and rose waters, if available.

Stir a little more until you have a pudding-like consistency.

Pour custard over rusk and syrup. Sprinkle with pistachios. Place in refrigerator for 5 hours, or leave it in overnight. Serve.

28 – Shaabiyat – Cream-Filled Pastries

This delicate dessert is easier to make when you use puff pastry, as I did here. It's full of cream filling and topped with a syrupy drizzle.

Makes 12 Servings

Cooking + Prep Time: 35 minutes

Ingredients:

- 1 pkg. of pastry, puff shells/cups
- Cream filling, prepared, 1 pkg., for filling & topping

To garnish:

- Pistachios, ground

For syrup:

- 1 cup of water, filtered
- 2 cups of sugar, granulated
- 1 tsp. of lime juice, fresh

Optional:

- Rose water & orange blossom water, if available
- Cinnamon stick(s) & vanilla extract, pure, as desired

Instructions:

To prepare syrup, add all ingredients to pan on med. heat. Stir well till syrup has thickened. Allow it to cool.

Bake puff pastry using the instructions on the package.

While pastry is still hot, drizzle with syrup.

Cut cups/shells in halves. Fill between with 1 tbsp. +/- of cream filling. Replace top parts.

Top filled shells/cups with 1 tbsp. each cream filling. Use crushed pistachios to garnish. Serve.

29 – Umm Ali – Bread Pudding

This dessert comes from the Middle East, but it's similar to bread pudding served in North America. It can be served while warm with ice cream, if you like.

Makes 8 Servings

Cooking + Prep Time: 45 minutes

Ingredients:

- 1 x 17 & 1/4-oz. pkg. of frozen/thawed pastry, puff
- 5 cups of milk, whole
- 1 cup of sugar, granulated
- 1 tsp. of vanilla extract, pure
- 1/4 cup of raisins, dark or golden
- 1/4 cup of almonds, slivered
- 1/4 cup of pistachio nuts, chopped
- 1/4 cup of coconut flakes, sweetened
- 1/4 cup of pine nuts

Instructions:

Preheat oven to 400F.

Unroll sheets of puff pastry. Place them flat on cookie sheet. Bake in 400F oven for 15 minutes, till golden brown and puffed.

Break pastry in pieces. Add them to large-sized bowl. Add coconut, pistachios, pine nuts, almonds and raisins. Toss, distributing nuts and fruits.

Pour mixture in 13" x 9" glass casserole dish. Spread out evenly.

Pour milk in a pan. Stir in vanilla and sugar. Heat till hot but not yet boiling. Pour over casserole dish mixture.

Bake in 400F oven for 15 minutes. Set oven on broil. Broil dish for two minutes, browning top. Remove from oven. Allow to stand for 5-7 minutes, then serve.

30 – Batheeth

This spice and date-based dessert is a favorite in the United Arab Emirates. It is typically served with coffee and can be served in balls or as crumbles.

Makes 10 balls

Cooking + Prep Time: 25 minutes

Ingredients:

- 8 & 3/4 oz of dates, deseeded
- 1/4 cup of water, filtered
- 1/4 cup of flour, wheat
- 2 tbsp. of unsalted butter, melted
- 1/4 tsp. of powdered cardamom
- 1/4 tsp. of powdered ginger

To coat, as desired:

- Sesame seeds, roasted
- Nut powder, coarse
- Coconut, desiccated

Instructions:

To prepare date paste, add water and dates to heavy pan. Heat on low. Press dates using a spatula. Press further and combine till the mixture has formed a paste. Let it cool a little.

To prepare batheeth, add flour in heavy pan. Place on low heat.

Roast flour, while stirring, till it has turned a golden brown in color.

You'll smell an aroma of nuttiness and smoke will start coming from pan. Remove pan from heat.

Add date paste & return pan to stove top burner over low heat.

Heat and combine mixture for 2 or 3 minutes, till you have a soft mixture. Flour should be mixed into date paste.

Add cardamom and ginger powders and combine well. Add the melted butter. Combine again. Remove pan from heat.

Allow mixture to cool a little so you can roll it into balls. Roll by hand into 1-tbsp. sized balls. Coat with coconut, seeds or nut powder, as desired. Serve with coffee.

Conclusion

This UAE cookbook has shown you…

How to use different ingredients to affect unique, Middle Eastern tastes in many dishes.

How can you include Emirati recipes in your home repertoire?

You can…

Make UAE breakfasts like shakshuka & chebabs, which you may not have heard of before. They are just as tasty for breakfast as they sound.

Cook soups, curries and stews, which are widely served in Emirati homes. Find ingredients in the produce or frozen food sections of your local grocery store.

Prepare tasty seafood dishes of the UAE, including shrimp and white fish. Fish is a mainstay in recipes year-round, and there are SO many ways to make it great.

Make dishes using lamb and beef in Middle Eastern meat-centered recipes. The meats make these dishes more filling and delicious.

Make Emirati desserts like bread pudding and pistachio truffles, sure to tempt anyone who enjoys sweets.

Share these wonderful recipes with all your friends!

About the Author

Allie Allen developed her passion for the culinary arts at the tender age of five when she would help her mother cook for their large family of 8. Even back then, her family knew this would be more than a hobby for the young Allie and when she graduated from high school, she applied to cooking school in London. It had always been a dream of the young chef to study with some of Europe's best and she made it happen by attending the Chef Academy of London.

After graduation, Allie decided to bring her skills back to North America and open up her own restaurant. After 10 successful years as head chef and owner, she decided to sell her business and pursue other career avenues. This monumental decision led Allie to her true calling, teaching. She also started to write e-books for her students to study at home for practice. She is now the proud author of several e-books and gives private and semi-private cooking lessons to a range of students at all levels of experience.

Stay tuned for more from this dynamic chef and teacher when she releases more informative e-books on cooking and baking in the near future. Her work is infused with stores and anecdotes you will love!

Author's Afterthoughts

I can't tell you how grateful I am that you decided to read my book. My most heartfelt thanks that you took time out of your life to choose my work and I hope you find benefit within these pages.

There are so many books available today that offer similar content so that makes it even more humbling that you decided to buying mine.

Tell me what you thought! I am eager to hear your opinion and ideas on what you read as are others who are looking for a good book to buy. Leave a review on Amazon.com so others can benefit from your wisdom!

With much thanks,

Allie Allen

Printed in Great Britain
by Amazon

25869790R00053